The Stars Above Us

The Stars Above Us

Poems by

Arvilla Fee

Cover design by Shay Culligan
Cover image by Jonathan Borba on Unsplash
Author photo by Arvilla Fee

ISBN: 979-8-90146-861-6

Kelsay Books
502 South 1040 East, A-119
American Fork, Utah 84003
Kelsaybooks.com

Dedicated to my husband, children, grandchildren,
parents, siblings, nieces, nephews, and wonderful friends.
I feel so incredibly blessed to have my life filled
with people who inspire me, encourage me,
and make it possible to be the best version of myself.

Acknowledgments

Thank you to the following publications, in which versions of these poems previously appeared:

The Amethyst Review: "Finding space"
The Blue Heron Review: "Not My Grandmother"
Blue Villa: "The Café Terrance at Night"
The Broken Teacup: "Paper Boats"
Cacti Fur: A Poetry High Ground: "The Irish Way," "Skipping"
Cholla Needles: "The Albatross," "Anti-Aging," "An Autumn Diagnosis," "The Best of Us," "The Collection Box," "The Dead Hours," "Exist," "I'm Made of Decisions," "Little Sister," "Lotus Flowers," "The Monks and I," "Musings of a Homeless Man," "Packing to Move," "Rewilding," "Salt Water," "Spool," "T Is for Tuesdays," "Time Warp," "To Shed a Season," "Triggers," "Unbendable," "Waiting for Rain," "What the Drought Leaves Behind," "When elephants cry"
Contemporary Haibun Online: "Summer's End"
Cool Beans Lit: "Gathering Minutes"
The Creekside Magazine: "The Button Jar"
Drifting Sands Haibun: "Aftermath," "The Flower Code," "Ripples," "Tradition,"
Duck Duck Mongoose Magazine: "The Beginning of Me"
Eunoia Review: "Not in the Same Way," "Not Ready"
Everscribe Magazine: "The Crack," "Summers Spent"
GAS: Poetry, Art, and Music: "The Air Between Us," "How to Eat an Over-Easy Egg in Front of Your Ex," "The Mad Librarian," "Momma Needs a Moment," "My dog will get me," "The Way You Waned"

The Green Silk Journal: "A Division of Goods"
The Hobo Journal: "Nature Speaks"
The Lake: "Words"
Last Leaves Magazine: "Just the Bare Bones," "She Wore Grief"
Libretto: "A Mother's Son"
Literary Heist: "Street Artist"
Literary Yard: "A Bicyclist in Amsterdam," "Dear Relatives," "Everything I Leave Behind," "Lunch Break"
Lothlorien Poetry Journal: "Aunt Josephine," "Circling," "One More Breath," "The Ritual of Loss," "When Frogs are Put to Bed"
Modern Literature: "A Garden Past," "Middle-Age Monotony," "Ornamental"
Monterey Poetry Review: "A Bending of Bones"
North of Oxford: "City Oasis," "Firefly, Firefly," "Ghost Cities," "The Ocean Gets Me," "Social Hoo Hahs,"
October Hill Magazine: "The Forecast," "Write it Again"
One Art: A Journal of Poetry (Work Anthology): "Working Hands"
The Orange Rose: "Didn't Make Headlines"
The Orchards Poetry Journal: "Afterthought," "Six-Hundred Days of January"
Paddler Press: "I left God"
Painted Pebble Lit Magazine: "Reprieve"
Panopoly: "Lessons from the Moon"
Paterson Literary Review: "A Way with Words"
Penstricken: "Roomba Rumble"

Poems for Tomorrow: "In spite of"
Poets' Espresso Review: "A Gypsy Soul," "The Lost Stories"
The Poetry Lighthouse: "Apartment Crossings," "Old Roads in Greece"
Rat's Ass Review: "My Grandma Knew"
The Ravens Perch: "Hibernation," "She Sang for Herself," "The Undoing of Maggie B," "Washed Away"
Remington Review: "Fragile Things," "Mother Days," "Winter's Gift," "You Should Have Been"
Right Hand Pointing (Ambidextrous Press): "Soldier Pieces"
Rusty Truck Press: "It's Not You," "Latitude and Longitude," "Time-Outs," "Vanished"
Rye Whiskey Review: "Coal Miners, 1933," "Stella Style"
Snakeskin: "An Unburdening"
Spillwords: "Ode to Autumn"
Stone Poetry Quarterly: "The Skin I'm In"
A Thin Slice of Anxiety: "The Brave Unbreakables," "Nonfiction"
Tipton Poetry Journal: "Keeper of the Clock," "No Filet Mignon for Me"
Verse-Virtual: "End of Harvest"
Wilderness House Literary Review: "From Room 312," "Momma Knew How"
Winged Penny Review: "My Father's Son," "Self-Care"
The Wise Owl: "In the Eye of the Storm"
Written Tales: "Winter Dream"
The Zest of the Lemon: "The Breathing Hours"

Contents

Part I. Weeping Stars

Part II: Traveling Stars

Part III: Reminiscing Stars

Part IV: Healing Stars

Part VI: Laughing Stars

Part I.

Weeping Stars

Aftermath

Inches, feet, walls of mud—slimy, thick, filled with debris. Houses flattened, splintered by the gnashing teeth of wind and rain. Battered hands comb through the wreckage, eyes red-rimmed with a thousand sorrows. How to pick up the pieces—pieces of homes, of hearts? Cries echo across palm fronds, pine forests, mountains, and valleys—one haunting refrain upon split lips: help us; in God's name, please help us! And strangers journey by boat, by plane, by truck, by mule . . . skimming across, flying over, trundling through the throttled lands, where rivers weep in city streets and weary voices cry out for food and water. It will take a miracle, they say, to bind up these jagged wounds that will no doubt bleed for ages, and yet, dots of hope appear, like tiny fireflies in twilight. Blinking. Blinking. Boxes. Bags. Crates. Cookouts. Carrying. Raking. Mopping. Sifting. Rescuing. Blinking. Blinking.

one smoky grill
a thousand fed hope
and hamburgers

Afterthought

I heard you visited the cemetery yesterday.
How do I know?
Little birds still chatter beyond the blue.
Someone said you bowed your head
but didn't speak.
Typical. Not really your style.
How long had we existed in silence?
Silence that grew like wild kudzu,
smothering everything good
beneath its viny sprawl—
that's the way of grudges I suppose,
when no one cares to prune.
I'm OK, though.
No apology necessary.
No need to pick up shears.

The Albatross

I carried a child in my womb,
bleached sun upon my head.
I thought her heavy at the time,
but I had not yet seen her grown.

Bleached sun upon my head,
pain cutting deep and low,
but I had not yet seen her grown,
the adult around my neck.

Pain cutting deep and low,
her words a scarlet red,
the adult around my neck,
my anchored albatross.

Her words a scarlet red;
she turned and slammed the door.
My anchored albatross,
too heavy for my grief.

She turned and slammed the door,
her words a scarlet red;
too heavy for my grief,
my anchored albatross.

An Autumn Diagnosis

They tell me I'll change,
lose weight,
lose hair,
fade like confetti leaves,
from golds and reds
to brittle brown.
I shall blow in the wind,
the tumble of me inevitable.
Winter will coat the ground
with its somber frost,
and I, too, shall grow blue
with autumn's last exhale
of breath.

A Bending of Bones

supple stretching,
back bends,
head stands
cartwheels,
the broken ones
heal
in an instant

subtle creaks,
a stiff uncurling
sitting to standing
standing to sitting,
a bit more unsure
of their place
in the body

scraping against
one another,
calcium on calcium,
as if they've forgotten
how to act;
they sniff out rain
and complain
when it comes

The Best of Us

The mice have eaten
through our memories,
shredded them,
shaped them into nests—

given birth to their young
on top of our yesterdays—

shedding droplets of blood
on what was once
the best of us.

Circling

If we were dogs, we'd sniff each other
        warily,
fur bristling on our necks, low growls
emanating from restricted throats.
        Instead,
we each take a long step back,
creating space and distance
        between two bodies
who once knew each other well.
We've been here before,
        you and I,
trading glances, each waiting
for the other to make a move.
        It's a macabre dance,
familiar, though neither of us
can remember the exact steps.
        Too many years
have passed since we vowed
to love each other
        till death do us part.
Too many promises lie broken
at our feet, like the china plates
        we hurled against the wall.
Truth is, we were *never* good together,
you and I, as evident by the way
        we now pass each other,
shoulders never touching.

The Crack

so thin, barely the width
of a whisker
across the floor;
neither of us see it at first—
a slightly faded smile,
one that doesn't quite reach
the eyes. But the crack grows
        w i d e r;
I think we both mention it
        in passing
as we hurry to our jobs,
backs bent against fraying nerves.
I'm not sure when we stumble home,
witness the chasm that has grown beneath
our calloused feet, but here we stand,
        you on one side
me on the other,
unsure how to bridge the gap.

The Dead Hours

cars screech around the bends
of country roads after midnight,
pavement black under a moonless
night—save for wedges of light
created by high beams; there's a
scurry of feet, bristled fur, eyes
frozen with shock as tires collide
with body—thwump, thwump—
then an eerie stillness, even the
wind holding its breath, awaiting
the outcome, but life has drained,
leaving eyes to stare blankly at the
star-pricked sky, ringed tail curled
around her body. She won't be alone;
daybreak will expose the carnage,
two opossums and a skunk,
splayed near her under a warming sun
where buzzards have begun to gather.

Didn’t Make Headlines

Betty Stump’s death notice
comes in an email

insipid corporate logo at the bottom
generic in the sense that it contains
a mere rib cage of facts—

her date of death
years of service at the newspaper
a perfunctory mention of her family

there are a few replies
sympathies and sad face emojis
the woman who works next to me

leans out around her monitor
whispers, *Who is Betty Stump?*
I shrug, a pinch of guilt caught

between my shoulder blades
my salon-gel nails still clacking
against the keyboard

Everything I Leave Behind

Do not weep, my darling,
as you lay me down;
I haven't gone that far;

I have flung my poems
into the stars,
see how they wink
conspiratorially
above your head,

I have planted words
in the aspens and the birches,
see how they sway
in every breeze
that brushes your cheeks

I have hidden words
in the early morning mist
that covers the valley,
see how they reveal themselves
as the sun crests the hills

I have given my words
to the monarch butterflies,
see how they land softly
on your extended hand
to let you know I'm still here

Exist

moving
from bed to toilet to bed

tottering
among ruins of a life once lived

attempting
to shut out persistent rays of sun

slurping
bits of Ramen to avoid starvation

sleeping
because to be awake is too much

to bear

The Flower Code

He hands me a bouquet, exquisite in both design and color, and smiles that benevolent smile. Or at least that's what most would think to see the slow grin spreading over even white teeth. Me—I see something different, something he reserves just for me. Malice. I accept the bouquet demurely with a slight bend of my head and make sure my voice is clear when I say, "Thank you." After he goes to the shower, I examine the bundle: baby's breath, everlasting love; honeysuckle, bonds of love; red salvia, forever mine. I get it. He's never going to let me go. Why would he when I've dutifully hidden his worst flaw for ten years with makeup and sunglasses. I arrange the stems in a vase; it's routine, habit, rote memory. The only change is imperceptible, a rapid increase in my heart rate because I know something he doesn't. Tomorrow these blooms will be upended in the trashcan, and a single strelitzia, "Bird of Paradise," will lie on the kitchen counter—freedom.

fissured ground
seeds skitter
in the wind

The Forecast

You brush my shoulder
in the confines
of the narrow kitchen;
we turn our heads
        in unison,
and I see clouds
gathering in the pupils
of your cold, gray eyes.
Calling for snow today,
        I deadpan;
you smirk and turn away.
I'm not sure
when we crossed the line,
when the last crusted leaf
        dropped
and left bare branches
twisting in the wind,
but I feel winter coming,
a deep chill settling
        into every bone.
Dinners will be spent
at opposite ends
of the table,
        and each word I utter
a step across the thickening ice
atop the lily pad pond.

Fragile Things

velvety wings
of a butterfly;
fresh-fallen
snowflakes,
perfection
upon the windowpane;
dandelion tufts
borne on the wind;
a sand dollar
gasping on the beach;
the cry of a newborn,
long and thin
like the whistle
of a midnight train;
tears marking
time in solitude;
a heart worn
upon a sleeve.

From Room 312

I watch the slow rise and fall
of his chest,
trusting the oxygen tube
to fill his lungs;
the church bells ring
when both clock hands
reach 12,
their peals sounding muted,
running like honey
down thickened glass.
For one brief moment
a purple pigeon lands
on the windowsill,
peers at me as if to ask
why I love my father so,
and I tell him in hushed whispers
that the man lying so thin in the bed
clothed in a speckled blue gown
has seen the best of me,
the worst of me
and has championed me
through it all.

In the Eye of the Storm

You touched me
where the bruise
was still fresh,
but I didn't flinch;
I sank into the purple
pool, resigned my fate
because what else
was there to do;
I was no one
without you,
as you'd reminded me
time and time again;
I kept phone numbers
tucked into the lining
of my purse,
tiny cards of hope
slipped to me
by do-gooders;
I took them out
sometimes
held them
like wishing stars
when you were out,
even tracing my fingers
over the lovely digits,
but I won't call, will I
because you'd know
and I'd never survive
the truth.

It's Not You

It's not you I fight against
when I awake,
my t-shirt soaked with sweat,
heart skittering out of my chest.
It's not your arm flung casually
across my stomach,
nor your legs entwined with mine.
It's the memory of another body—
the one who ground me down to powder
and left me in the wind.

Keeper of the Clock

I kept schedules, itineraries, calendars—
dates and times stood at attention

when I entered a room; to-do lists shrank
against the grating edge of my black pen

then there was you—reveling in spontaneity,
going with the flow, a casual flip of your braid

eye rolls, long sighs warring against my watch,
always two steps behind, ten minutes too late—

until you weren't—until I answered a knock,
and two officers solemnly stood, hats in hands,

until the words *we regret to inform* you pierced
my brain, wrenched a scream from my throat;

numbers and hands exploded from the face
of the clock, every shard cutting my tender feet;

how could the sun and moon continue to trade
places now that time lay perpetually stagnant,

now that I lay prone on top of your yellow quilt
wishing you hadn't swallowed the calendar whole?

A Mother's Son

Don't send officers to my door;
don't say you regret to inform me.
I don't want a 21-gun salute
or taps played on a trumpet
or a triangle-folded flag.
I don't want to visit a white cross
and stare at the ground
where an empty casket encases
a single set of dog tags.
I don't want the words,
Remains were not recoverable
to represent a boy
who loved to make mud pies
and wrestle with his sisters
and climb apple trees
and pick wildflowers for my table.
I asked you to keep him safe,
and though you made no promises,
I expected to welcome him back
with open arms—and now my arms
will never feel his muscled weight;
my heart alone must carry the stone.
Don't tell me time heals all wounds.

Musings of a Homeless Man

The discarded cheese is a little off,
but I eat it anyway
because it's slightly better than
yesterday's week-old bread—
besides the mouse didn't bat an eye
when I gave him the first bite.

Nonfiction

I laid myself in your outstretched hands,
the pages splayed to Chapter One.
My only wish—that you would cherish the pages,
turn them one-by-one, let every word
become a seed on fertile soil.
You smiled, but your hands were hurried,
anxious, I think, to read ahead,
and so you brushed past my background,
all those little moments that shaped me,
built me into the human I am today.
I thought it wouldn't matter, but you skipped
so much, reading only the parts you liked,
dog-earing the part where you came in.
I suppose that could have been romantic,
but you thumbed through my tears,
those times I felt misunderstood,
because, as you said, you've never been big
on drama. If only you had slowed down,
had taken the time to lose yourself
in my vulnerability—I promise
you would have read that chapter again
and again. But you wanted to reach the end,
to say you'd read it all—when, in fact,
the entire plot was lost on you.
You didn't see it coming, that last page,
when I turned my back and closed the door.

Not Ready

The universal force,
or perhaps time itself
pulls the hands
of the clock,
forces it to strike
the hour—
but I'm not ready
for your departure,
not ready to sift
through boxes
of photographs,
to keep a remnant
of your voice
in a message
on my phone.
I can't bear the thought
of vacant shoes
tucked under a bare bed,
bare—save for the imprint
of where you used to be.
There's no self-help book
to prepare me for your loss—
no *How to Lose Your Parents*
for Dummies resting on a shelf.
I wouldn't read it anyway,
for I cannot bring myself
to shine a light in the cracks

you'll leave when you're gone.
Can't bear to rub my tongue,
like I did when just a child,
along the vacant spot of gum
where a solid tooth once stood.

Paper Boats

I first caught sight of you
down at the river's edge,
you with your tousled
hair and crooked grin;
you had a paper boat,
and it was sailing along
as if it were made
of much sterner stuff,
and I looked at you in awe,
looked at the boat in awe;
I'd never seen paper
survive in water before;
so, perhaps that's how
we ended up, you and I,
engaged,
married,
having a child—
because I thought
you could make paper
float; thought you could take
something of little substance
and make it sail a pirate's sea,
but you didn't know how
to take the paper of us,
shape it,
waterproof it,
set it upon water;
so, we shredded
into a million soggy pieces
and stuck to the sides
of the muddy bank.

Ripples

I cast a stone into the pond, watch the rings widening, widening, widening. That's how I got here, I think. A stone. Thrown into a pond. And here I am, on the cusp of the widest ring, watching it spread.

New York City, my job as an editor. Yellow taxis. Shoulder-to-shoulder pedestrians. The smell of exhaust and hot dog stands. High rises. Pigeons. How I love the buzz of it all.

The smooth, dove-gray walls of a doctor's office. A doctor with fingers steepled in front of him on his mahogany desk. The diagnosis: cancer. Chemo. Radiation. Six months at best.

Our farm, that is to say, Mom and Dad's farm. The return to country air. Hay and clover. A different kind of buzz strummed out across the fields by the pollen-laden legs of bees. The rat-tat-tat of a woodpecker. And the pond. The stones. The broken surface of water meant to be still.

crumbling bank
white canvas shoes
marked with mud

The Ritual of Loss

the unearthly silence
that follows the *call—*
the call that splits time
into then and now,
going-through-the-motions,
the planning,
catalogues of caskets,
browsing for designs, prices
as though looking
for a new fall wardrobe,
the service, mourners'
tears and well-wishes;
I'm sorry for your loss
blankets the landscape
of each raw nerve
of eyes swollen red
of a throat too tight to speak,
and then it's over—
flowers donated,
thank you cards in the mail,
bank accounts and bills tended,
closets cleaned, memories sorted
into piles of junk
and forget-me-nots

Salt Water

After Rolf Edberg

Dome above, bowl beneath,
sky and sea joined at the hip,
bodies of blue entwined
just as we once were;
no one can tell where one begins
and the other ends.
The smell of salt fills my nose,
its heady scent reminiscent
of our limbs slick with sweat,
passion pressed between sheets.
Many do not understand
why I still come here,
why I love the imprint of sand
on my tanned thighs,
why I pretend your guitar calluses
are still playing notes against my skin.
But it's here, with gulls screeching,
as I slip my fingers into a bag of grapes
that I feel you most.
You are that burst of sour-sweet juice,
the sanguine sunshine
tinting my cheeks blush-pink.
It's here I can float on my back,
buoyed by the beautiful evocation
of our foreheads bowed toward each other,
our lips searching for salt.

She Wore Grief

like mustard,
        tangy
bitter
        dull yellow;
she hurled prayers
at heaven's gates,
        questions
shaped like   why?
she waited—
the answer came
        in thunder
in lightening
        in spatters
of raindrops
the answer came
        with a voice
if you hadn't loved
        you would not feel
the loss.

Skipping

You became the voice
inside my head
like an old 45,
needle stuck in a groove

you're not good enough
you're not good enough

I had no one
to lift the needle,
to play the rest of the song,
and so I spun round and round
inside those lyrics.

Soldier Pieces

His hands shake
as I pass him the bowl,
his eyes darting
from side-to-side.
I speak gently to him,
like a negotiator
poised on a windowsill
coaxing a man
from the ledge.
He relaxes for a moment,
sucks in a deep breath,
releases it,
picks up his fork.
His face looks the same—
half shadows, half flame
from the candles I'd lit;
yet I know it isn't.
There are worry lines
etched into his brow,
framing the corners
of his mouth,
his once bright smile.
There is a guardedness,
one I must accept
as I gather the pieces
to help make him whole.

Spool

You pulled,
unwound every piece of me,
thread unmoored from its core.
I gathered myself,
began the trip back—
around and around
to find my center.
I'm reattached now,
not in unruffled perfection,
but a looser version
of one who has known
the misery of being undone.

T Is for Tuesdays

why do such extraordinary things
happen on Tuesdays—
not the beginning
nor the end,
but an average middle day
on which people decide
to exit the world
on which an unexpected phone call
comes too late to say goodbye;
on which crosses
are planted in the earth,
forever the lowercase t

Unbendable

You are hard to love,
and I don't think you know.
You can't see the rough bark
grown around your exterior,
how it chafes my palm
when I try to touch you;
you can't see how the wind
in my conversational breath
presses with all its might
against unyielding branches.
You weren't always this way;
there was a time of supple limbs,
green—flexible between my fingers,
a time of heads pressed together,
bodies fitting notch-for-notch,
a time when I didn't ache
under your canopy of leaves.

Vanished

You disappeared
like the remnants
of a dream
upon waking.
Only fragments
          remain—
a coffee mug
permanently stained
in the bottom,
t-shirts that carry
your ocean scent,
an acoustic guitar,
a half-written song
on a notecard.
If I lie in bed
and close my eyes,
I can almost grasp
the unabridged version
of you
before it slips like smoke
through my fingers.

The Way You Waned

So round and full were you,
a beaming smile
upon your face,

the kind to wine and dine
and cast your light
around a room;

your gravity pulled me,
a tide so high
I lost myself

until you grew thinner,
then thinner still,
a mere razor

I could no longer hold
lest it leave a scar.

When elephants cry

one has fallen,
too young they say,
so much life unlived,
and the elders huddle,
pressing into one another's
shoulders as if it takes all bodies
to stand, to wail, to pour their grief
upon the ground. They won't leave now.
They will bury their dead and mourn the bones.

Write It Again

If I handed you our story,
having erased all the pages,
would you rewrite the script?
Would you take the empty space
as an opportunity
to pen an apology,
to right the capsized ship,
to see your role in our demise?
Or would you fill it up again
with a thousand little injuries,
wounds that turned the pages red?

You Should Have Been

a flame thrower
a magician
a used-car salesman
a black jack dealer in Vegas,

for all your pizzazz,
audaciousness,
charisma,
and duplicity,

for your careless handling
of the truth,
for your slick-backed tongue
sliding compliments
into unsuspecting purses,
for your treacherous eyes
that wink in broad daylight,

you should have been anything
but a husband.

Part II:

Traveling Stars

Apartment Crossings

The man in the brown tweed coat
nods to the jogger in green leggings,
she nods back, adjusts her ponytail,
bounces on the balls of her feet
then waves to the old lady from 109
who has the three-legged cat;
the old lady says, *the sun's out,*
turns to the mechanic with half-moons
of grease around each of his nails,
and repeats, *the sun's out.*
The mechanic grins, says he can sleep
rain or shine—steps into the elevator,
where Mr. Brisket (not his real name;
he just cooks a lot of brisket)
is tapping a newspaper against his palm.
They ride to the fifth floor and are met
by the eight-year-old twins from 507
just as the doors open. They high-five Brisket
and ask for peppermints, which he doles out
of the pockets of his red-paisley robe.
Katarina strides down the hallway
in cargo pants and combat boots,
stopping only to give the group a salute.
No one knows if she's *actually* military,
but her cropped hair and impossibly straight
posture leave people to wonder.
She exits the building; Mrs. Allbright,
coming back from the beauty parlor
with freshly-coiffed blue hair
tells her there's a chance of rain,
late afternoon.

Aunt Josephine

My aunt was a fearsome creature,
all stiff posture and inescapable gray bun.
Born in the wrong era, I suppose,
for she would've made a splendid Victorian.
As a child, I respected her in that way children
respected all adults with such chiseled features.
I admired her, too, the way she could sit
for an hour-long sermon without breaking a sweat.
We cousins would cast sidelong glances,
each in on the bet as to what auntie would do
should a fly buzz in through the open windows
and land on her steepled vein-mapped hands.
None ever did though; I suspect they dared not.
Because even the gumtrees held their sticky breath
until auntie rose like a pillar of fire for the final prayer.

A Bicyclist in Amsterdam

I wait at the crosswalk—
cars and bicycles hurtling past,

a cacophony of bodies,
metal and human flesh,

a tableau of chaos, and yet
there, in the hurried midst . . .

a lady in a green dress,
pedaling her bike,

nearly ethereal,
emerald silks billowing,

back erect, chin tilted.
I envy her finesse,

the little wooden basket
that holds her groceries.

I try to imagine myself
on that same bike,

effortlessly navigating
cobblestone and traffic

—but I’m wearing jeans
and a t-shirt, standing,

a clumsy American tourist,
bikeless since childhood.

The Café Terrace at Night

It was closing time at the Van Gogh Museum
in Amsterdam, but I didn't want to leave,
so, I slipped inside the Café Terrace—
thought of no better place to spend the night.
I weaved through the tables, listened to people
chatting amiably, the night alluringly warm
with a gentle breeze, stars blazing like lanterns
in a sky of azure blue. Delightful smells drifted
out of the café—garlic, butter, yeasty breads.
I took a seat at one of the empty tables, watched
a lady stroll past, dressed in lemon-drop yellow,
and marveled at the way the café lights dotted
the blue-lilac paving stones with enchanting
flecks of gold. I thought of crossing the street,
popping into the corner store with its lights on,
but I stayed, ordered some wine, a breadbasket
and cheese—absolutely divine. Then I retired
to a room upstairs, overlooking the café. I'm sure
Van Gogh would have happily painted me leaning
out an open window, had I not been so bold
as to wear my red satin nightgown.

End of Harvest

Gramps and I walk into Tommy's, a little dive in Chattanooga with greasy food, the best-tasting beer, and a beat-up juke box that still takes quarters. This place is among the few that still lets people smoke, and Gramps lights up soon as he walks in. We plop down on sticky leather bar stools, worn and cracked with time, denim-clad butts and liquor. He orders a whiskey, I order a stout and light up my own cig. Gramps frowns, says just 'cause he does it, doesn't make it right. I nod and don't say his influence has shaped my very bones—don't tell him he's the biggest, best giant I've ever known, and how I hope to be *exactly* like him when I'm 82—part of the rich soil, fingers crusted with its marrow, body aching from head to toe after bringing in the crops that me and God grew from seed. But—maybe I *should* tell him. I lean into his shoulder, start into my praise-be monologue, but he just raises his glass and peers silently at me beneath his bushy white eyebrows until I raise my bottle. "Good harvest. 'Nuff said," Gramps says, his mouth twitching at the corners. I tap his glass and grin. He never was much on making a fuss.

A Gypsy Soul

I loved her as any daughter would,
loved her red-orange skirts and bangles,

the way she tinkled like a hundred bells
when she cooked bacon, eggs and grits,

the way she twirled when she swept the floor,
as if every chore was a dance, something

to be celebrated with song and cheer,
but I saw the careful way my father watched her,

his deep brown eyes reflecting pools of fear;
I suppose he knew her best, knew her love

of scarves and jewels and sparkly things,
knew her restless legs would one day

skip out into the wider world, but he held her
for a while; I held her for a while—each of us

attached to supple hips that swayed to music
only she could hear.

The Irish Way

She didn't own the bar,
but she *owned* the bar,
if you know what I mean,
the Irish red-haired beauty
with light freckled skin
and a laugh like windchimes.
She could handle a cloth,
a mug, a till full of money,
a compliment, a come-on,
bleary eyes, and brawling fists
as if she were born
in the bar's storeroom.
As if she'd cut her teeth
on the legs of the stools,
had drunk milk from the taps.
She moved like a dancer,
her eyes never leaving
a single person out of view.
People respected her
like they respected priests
and little old ladies,
equally awed
and terrified.
I had my first and last fight
in that bar—had felt the pinch
of her strong fingers,
had landed on my backside
just beyond the door.

And when I'd apologized,
she'd looked down and quoted
Richard Braunstein's statement
that a bartender must figure out
who is drunk
and who is just stupid.
Then she said, *Which
do you want to be?*
I'd laughed and told her
I'd rather be drunk.
Then she'd winked,
and closed the door.

The Mad Librarian

Everyone said he was crazy,
my grandfather,
but I liked to think of him as
unconventional.
OK—so maybe the five hens
that slept in old milk crates
on his front porch was a little crazy.
Maybe the life-size garden statue
of Edgar Allan Poe with a raven
sitting on his head was—
well, odd at best.
But the pinnacle of his peculiarity,
according to the wholesome folks in town,
was his insatiable love of books.
Having converted his 1920-something
house into a massive library
when I was just a kid,
I found the rows and rows of bookcases
perfectly normal! Little books, big books,
books that smelled like the earth itself,
books with water marks and wax seals.
Books with red covers, brown covers,
no covers at all—tattered pages clinging
desperately to the threads that bound them.

Grandfather often sat in a winged back chair,
a book perched upon his knee, a book open
on his lap, a book held between two gnarled hands,
his gold, wire-rimmed glasses perched smartly
on the end of his thin nose.
I stepped on his glasses once, breaking both lenses,
but he kept reading with them anyway,
said it gave him a whole new perspective.
And it's those glasses, sitting demurely on the last stack
of books he read that now waver behind the salty film
of tears in my eyes. I blink twice, put the specs on my face,
trying to see through Grandfather's eyes.

The Monks and I

Black boulders jut from the earth,
round, uneven teeth
stark against a robin-egg sky.
A speck perches on the edge
of a cliff—
a bird's nest from ground view,
a monastery up close.
There's a pureness here—
of air
of water
of soil
of soul.
Legs bathed in the silkiest skirt,
I sink into the softness
of this holy place,
yielding to an undercurrent
begging me to rest.

Not My Grandmother

I gently take the withered hands
of the white-haired lady
who sits, shoulders hunched forward,
in her wheelchair.
Her faded cornflower-blue eyes
take me in, widening just a bit
in gleeful recognition.
Good morning, Claire, I whisper,
and she grins, displaying a few
vintage gold-capped teeth.
I have a secret, she whispers back,
and I lean forward to listen,
knowing this is one of her favorite
games—*I took an extra pudding*
from the food cart, she says.
I giggle and lightly touch her nose.
Good for you, you little devil.
Want to hear another secret? She asks.
I nod—and we sit like this for hours.
Her family thinks she's lost,
too mentally out of it
to engage in conversation;
they only visit once a year.
But I come every week,
not out of obligation,
but because Claire is a gift
that should be unwrapped
more often than holidays.

Old Roads in Greece

Dusty were the feet that tread upon these stones,
stones now worn with time and age and ripened rain.
If I were to rub them with my fingers, remove today's
soil, would I unearth a Roman soldier, clad as he was
in breastplate, helmet, and spear? Would I rub against
the worshipers who came bearing gifts for Zeus?
If I got down on my knees, pried ancient soil from between
the cracks, would I hear the sound of chariots, the thrum
of hardened feet racing for a laurel crown? Come to me,
Grecian ladies laden with jewels and scarves, brush my lips
with your olive oils, and let me kiss the history
now carved into my heart.

Ornamental

The cobblestones are warm beneath my sandaled feet,
stores with open faces beckon me in to touch, to *feel.*

I smile at the easy, eager voices, *Come in. Come in!* Each
welcoming me with open arms, not as foreigner but friend.

I sweep in and out of shops, my senses sharpened by colors,
my arms soon laden with jewelry, blankets, and amber honey.

I purchase not *things* but memories, each richly steeped
like tea bags in Grecian mountain air. I look up at the oranges,

round bulbs hanging from lush-leaf trees that border streets.
I would pick one, if not for the words of a Greek guide: *No good,*

she says,   *only decoration*   *fruit is sour*   *you not like.*
But I *do* like—these wonderful, useless oranges that offer nothing

but the evening ocher glow cast by an ancient sun.

Stella Style

Stella wasn't young anymore,
but you could tell she'd been
a real beauty back in her day.
She was also tough as nails.
Ain't *nobody* talking back to
that woman! I'd seen her fury
first-hand when a foul-mouthed
drunk decided to push a woman.
Lordy, Stella charged at him with
the ferocity of a long-horned bull.
Put his back against the wall.
As a regular at Caddy's, I'd stop
in for a beer at the end of a long
haul, my trucking time taking a toll
on my limbs. And there she'd be,
Stella, black tank, lotus tattoo
on the back of her lean shoulder,
wiping the bar with a white rag,
shooting the bull with patrons,
pulling those taps like a champ.
I asked her one day why she did it—
why, after *all* these years, she wanted
to put up with roughnecks and drunks
and young punks like me. She'd thrown
her head back and laughed, said since
she'd never been able to have children,
she figured she'd plant herself in the one
place where everyone needed a mother.

Street Artist

I like the blue of you;
you're using ultramarine today,
and I smile to see sloppy half moons
curved around the edges
of your blunt fingernails.
You don't see me—or at least
not anymore than you see anyone else
who has gathered to watch you paint.
But I see *more* than the painting,
your rendition of a gauzy summer sky
arched over a crumbling brick wall,
which is covered in ivy that spreads
like a coup d'état.
I see wayward strands of raw umber
hair fall across your eyes, the way you
tap the handle of the paintbrush
against your bottom lip when you are thinking,
the faded, low-slung jeans with a hole in one knee,
the black t-shirt with cut-off sleeves.
I follow the flick of your wrist,
the sweeping brush strokes
that blend the very bones of you,
and think I might   someday
hang a piece of your soul on my wall.

The Undoing of Maggie B

Maggie slips out of the hospital gown,
pulls on her silk blouse and skirt,
and backs out of the frigid room
with its antiseptic smells and tiled floors;
her heels click past the ER front desk,
and she inhales the scent of coming rain
as the exit doors open with a swoosh;
she wipes trails of mascara
from beneath red-rimmed eyes,
gets into the driver's side of her car,
puts it in reverse, and takes the roads—
        back to the hotel
        back to the charity fund-raiser
        back to her boss with the debonair smile
she sidesteps his arm—melts into the crowd,
hobnobs with the giggling, glitter-bright donors,
        is never alone,
        is never pulled into a room,
        is never a gazelle before a lion;
she is safe and blissfully unbroken.

A Way with Words

Oh, how he could talk,
that slick-tongued used car
salesman. He gesticulated,
ran his fingers down the pearl
snap buttons of his blue plaid
shirt, tapped the gritty pavement
with his snakeskin boots.

He puffed out his chest
like a golden blowfish,
pontificating about the 1975
Oldsmobile Cutlass
(now twelve years old)—
its powerful V8, its sleek design,
coolest car on the road!

My dad folded his arms across
his chest, stoically silent.
The car would be mine, one I'd drive
to college and beyond—and
he was waiting to see what I'd do,
to see if I'd wheel and deal
like he'd taught me.

But the dealer seemed to grow larger
with each gesture, his thick black hair

puffing like smoke from an exhaust pipe.
Dad harrumphed about the price, but
waited; so, I straightened to my five foot ten,
said: "I'll take a look, make you an offer."
The man blinked in surprise.

Then I lifted the hood, ran my hands across
its engine, checked the oil, kicked the tires,
checked the brakes, inspected the interior,
took it for a test drive. "I'll give you $2,000."
The man looked at my dad. Guess he'd never
had a girl make him an offer. Dad shrugged.
"Take it or leave it," I said. He took it.

Working Hands

I stare at Dad's hands
perched on my teacher's desk
like two plump pigeons
and my cheeks flush hot;
Dad is wearing his best blue shirt
and a pair of unripped jeans,
but he couldn't clean his nails?
Not even for a conference?
Grease, the labor of a thousand cars,
lies under each nail, black half moons
shedding inky light on the lives we lead—
single trailer, cracked kitchen counters,
a front door that never shuts
without a shove from the hip.
My teacher smiles and shakes Dad's hand,
her creamy skin like fine silk stockings
against his burlap palms.
At home, Dad cooks steaks for dinner,
and as he cuts the tender pieces,
he nods to my plate and says,
that was a '57 Chevy.

Part III:

Reminiscing Stars

The Button Jar

little buttons,
big buttons,
brown, pink, cream,
aqua, black, ochre,
buttons covered with cloth,
buttons with two holes,
four holes;
I ask my grandmother
why she has so many buttons
in one jar—tell her no one can use
that many buttons in a lifetime,
but she says she's used three such jars
in her lifetime and will, at age 68,
undoubtedly use at least one more.
But where do they go? I ask.
She points to the dolly on my lap,
two large black buttons for eyes.
She presses her fingertips
against the back of my blue cotton dress,
making her way down
each of the six navy buttons.
She picks up my coat, Grandpa's coat,
her own coat, and taps each set,
canary yellow, earthy brown, and clear.
Smiling, she leads me to the kitchen,
lifting a tea towel from the drawer.
I grin back—it has a single seafoam button
sewn on its crocheted top, meant to fasten it

to the handle of a stove.
The thing about buttons, she says,
is they live intriguing lives, often traveling
from a dress to suspenders, to a horse blanket.
If you pay attention, you'll see them everywhere.
Back in her sewing room,
she lets me tip the full Mason jar on its side,
and I run my hand through the delightful pile,
feeling the weight of a button's importance
for the very first time.

Coal Miners, 1933

In a little blues bar
in a little blue town
cigarette smoke
encircled his head,
a most unangelic halo,
but he kept his eyes closed,
lips pressed to the reed
of that silver Selmer sax.
Its deep-throated notes
hung like tinsel
in the too-warm air
just above the blackened heads
of those who guzzled away
the dust and grit
of another lungless day
beneath shrouded ground
where there is no sun
and canaries go to die.

The Collection Box

Mom sits in her favorite chair, a blue and white paisley with a matching ottoman. Its arms are faded from her bony elbows positioned in the same tired places when knitting, reading, doing crosswords, sipping cups of chamomile tea. She watches me warily as I lift the edges of papers on an end table, peer into a cardboard box, examine the dust on the mantle. To clean, really clean, I'd need to rent a dumpster. But I can't. I'd thrown away some junk years ago, and that's when Mom had *the talk* with me. Not the birds and bees talk. I was married with kids. But the do-not-throw-away-my-life talk. Gesturing to her piles of quilting scraps, jars of buttons, Pop's old carpenter tools, foam boxes from a farm where she used to gather eggs, old flower pots my brother and I had painted, placemats embroidered by her sister, Nell, she'd said, *Everything here is a piece of me. I may not be able to tell you what I had for dinner yesterday, but all of this* (she'd opened her arms wide) *I've lived a thousand times, and I intend to go on living it a thousand more.*

a gray mouse sleeps
its nest lined
with treasure

Dear Relatives

Just look at all of you, now that Gran is gone,
hands pawing through fragile wedding quilts.
It's too late to fall in love with rosebud china now;
you were all too busy to drink her ginger tea.

Hands pawing through fragile wedding quilts
not one of you deserves a block or scrap.
You were all too busy to drink her ginger tea,
her golden stories blurred as you rushed past.

Not one of you deserves a block or scrap;
you weren't around when Gran lost her curly hair.
Her golden stories blurred as you rushed past;
every finger itching to hold the family trust.

You weren't around when Gran lost her curly hair;
it's too late to fall in love with rosebud china now.
Every finger itching to hold the family trust;
look at all of you, now that Gran is gone.

A Division of Goods

When grandma passed
oh, you should have seen
how the children, grandchildren,
cousins, aunts and uncles
fought over her possessions.

She wasn't rich by any means,
but she had stuff—you know,
collectibles, antiques, pictures,
a set of china (which may have
been worth something).

But the way they carried on,
well, you would have thought
they stood to gain millions,
and it soon became a contest
about whom was the closest,

who knew her best, who she'd
want to have this thing or that,
and I let them squabble
because all I wanted was one
teaspoon, the one she'd used

every day to stir her hot tea,
the silver one with a flat handle,
the one she would lick remnants
of honey from before setting it
beside her cup on a saucer.

So, I took that one spoon;
I don't think anyone noticed.
Today I stir my tea, savor the
honey, and she's sitting here,
grinning like the Cheshire Cat.

Firefly, Firefly

I exit my car,
immediately regretting
the absence of my A/C.
Grams won’t have air either,
just a couple of creaky box fans
that are probably older than me.
As I walk towards her porch,
I spot a tiny yellow light—it blinks
off, on—off, on, and suddenly,

I’m nine years old again,
a blue Bell jar in one hand,
the other hand out stretched,
running in dizzying circles
chasing fireflies—
wink over there, blink over here.
Tall blades of grass bristle against
my suntanned legs, and my hair
has sprouted wings in the humidity,
but I won’t stop running until the jar
looks like a fairy lantern.

Grams steps out and greets me
with a smile. Then she recites softly
in her sing-song voice I know so well:

"Firefly, Firefly
blinking in the twilight sky,
come give my finger a gentle kiss,
please grant me just one little wish."
I smile up at her, memories leaking
from my eyes.

A Garden Past

I should have known
when blooms wilted
then dropped like confetti,
when leggy weeds sprang up
to swallow both rain and sun

that there was no coming back
from the brambles;
the garden we once tended gone—
now grown wild with accusations

soil barely clinging to roots, rot-bitter
with beetle bites and half-spun truths.
If possible, I'd start over,
dig out every last stem and leaf

till up the past, turn topside down
let earthworms regurgitate each clump
and create something new.

Ghost Cities

lie along the freeways,
limp as dishcloths;
people speed past
casting cursory glances
at plywood covered windows,
soulless eyes long dead—
after the great migration,
after factories closed,
after stocks took a nosedive,
after steel turned into stone,
only those with feet wedged
beneath the poverty line remain—
to prop up leaning gutters and
toss rocks at rusted-out cars
that adorn their brittle lawns,
          ashtrays full,
                    whiskey bottles empty

Little Sister

I grew up
in your shade
never quite touching
the sunlight
as your branches
were full of leaves
and birds sang
full-throated songs
from your depths,
and so I learned
to create clever paths
in the forest.

The Lost Stories

I wish I could gather up stories,
nestle them in a wicker basket

among puffy skeins of wool,
but I never met my grandfather

on my father's side—nor grandmother,
and my careless youth tossed aside

my father's book of assorted tales,
as she had more important things to do,

and so, here I sit, at the side of the ocean
crying into my sieve as the stories wash out

with the tide.

Momma Knew How

Momma knew how
to cut a log of bologna
into paper-thin slices,
how to stretch
powdered laundry soap
to wash one more load,
how to turn bottles
upside down—
use that last drop
of cooking oil,
how to make
a sliver of Irish Spring
clean us for a week,
how to dig our *empty* tubes
of toothpaste out of the trash
and squeeze them to death
for at least a dozen brushes.
She never complained,
never asked anyone for a dime,
not even when Pop left,
drink getting the best of him,
not even when she worked
doubles at the diner.
She never needed more
than an 8th-grade education;
she just knew how
to spin straw into gold.

Mother Days

The maple tree provides the most shade,
and it is there I spread my blanket
and arrange the contents of my picnic basket
(ham salad sandwiches, pickles, olives,
thick slices of cheddar cheese, strawberries,
and homemade peanut butter cookies)
onto decorative paper plates.
I place the jar of sun tea on a flat piece of ground,
intent on keeping it out of reach of the children.
Then I hear the pounding of feet.
Even though I haven't rung the bell,
the children seem to know each hour of the day
when food is served,
as if bells reside inside their stomachs
rather than at the end of the wooden handle I now hold.
They giggle, flop onto the blanket in little piles
of ripped jeans and t-shirts.
Ranging in ages from five to nine years old,
their voices rise to a fevered pitch
as they examine the items on their plates
before cramming bites of food into their mouths.
I smile at them,
these four delightful, infuriating beings
who call me mom,
who drive me completely mad,
who hung the moon and stars.

My Grandma Knew

Jesus
how to can tomatoes,
how to catch more flies with honey,
how to use the sun ball as a clock

she knew camp fires,
tin cans cut open with knives,
that moss mostly grew
on the north side of trees

she knew how to sing
"The Devil Went Down to Georgia"
and how to play the fiddle
that'd put Johnny boy to shame

She knew red morning skies
meant rain was coming,
she knew shelling peas
and thumping melons,

ghost stories in the night,
half-truths and outright lies,
she knew how to hold a girl-sized hand
when life went a little sideways.

Packing to Move

I didn’t realize,
until I tried to unearth you,
tried to pull up your stubborn roots,
that you are bound by memories,
inexorably tangled
by bits and baubles of the past:
fishing lures, ancient blades,
a jar of screws, balls of twine,
misshapen hats, dusty boots,
a box of rusty tools.
Not a single thing is trash,
not to you,
and to pry possessions
from desperate hands
is to break the very joints
that hold the form together.

Summer's End

He stares at the ground. Scuffs his feet like a school boy caught going down the playground slide head first. His face is flushed in the late August sun, perhaps from our hours spent on the floating dock, perhaps from embarrassment. I don't say anything. A deliberate choice. I know my silence will drive him mad. Plus, I have nothing to say. He'd said it all earlier. He was going off to college. No sense keeping up a relationship surely doomed to fail given the distance and time apart. I'd seen it coming. The hints of pulling away. The gaps in conversation. Averted eyes when I'd mentioned seeing him fall break. But I'd put it off as dread on his part, fooling myself as long as I could. But here we are. End of the line as they say. I can no longer fool anyone, least of all myself. He leans in for an awkward hug, but I hold my arms stiffly at my sides so that he bumps against my hip bone like a body meeting a fence post. *I'm sorry,* he murmurs, his lips close to my ear. I nod, turn, close the door to my house with a deafening click.

pieces of photographs
there's no shame
in confetti

Summers Spent

our hair limp with sweat, sweet tea
passing our lips, dribbling down
parched throats—the most
complicated construct, cats in
the cradle, our hands entwined
with string. We hum along to
Beatles' songs on a scratchy
cassette player as bees sip nectar
from cups of purple clover. We
know nothing of adulting, not yet,
we only know fresh white bread,
bologna, and mustard smiley
faces; we know how rain tastes on
the tongue, how cool mud feels
after a cloud-burst of rain. And we
laugh and dance as though
childhood is an endless
commodity, without expiration,
without guilt.

Time Warp

I stop at an old diner
somewhere out west—

nondescript town
nondescript dust.

A bell over the door tinkles
cross a threshold into 1952—

cracked red-leather-topped stools
with wobbly chrome legs,

same raw red at each booth,
black and white linoleum floor

that has seen its share
of cobbled boots and truckers.

Order a plate of over-easy eggs,
with biscuit and jelly on the side

from a waitress named Betty,
probably once a buxom blonde

but now wears support hose
and an apron tied loosely

around her middle-aged middle.
She calls me honey, though

and refills my coffee three times,
which makes up for the dead flies

lining the window ledge.

Tradition

The sun hangs one hour above the ocean, an orange ball pulsating with the syncopated rhythm of weathered hands slapping skins stretched taut over bongos and congas—ta-dum, ta-dum. The beat elicits gyrations, primal urges heeled and toed into sugary sand. Skirts jingle with gypsy wishes; bare chests glisten with inkwells of memories. Wide grins flash around the circle—dreadlocks, flip flops, hula hoops, butterfly wings—ta-dum, ta-dum, ta-dum; arms twist and twine like snakes, glowing faces turned toward the red-orange blaze. The sun hangs two minutes above the ocean. A bronzed man steps forward, blows the conch—whommm—whommmmm.

collective pulse
the sun slips through
the fingers of time

Washed Away

It floods like a river bursting
the boundaries of its banks,
swallowing farms and fields,
tapping at desperate doors.
It floods like a basement floor,
unsettling trim and drywall,
blotting out children's histories
stored in quaintly colored totes.
It floods like dam, cracked
by years of neglect,
by apologies left unsaid,
by sheets now grown cold.
It floods like a sewer,
spewing waste into streets
clogged by the broken ones,
covering hand-painted signs:
I will work for food.
It floods like tear ducts
suppressed far too long,
dislodges the lump
wedged inside the throat.
It floods like an argument,
words heaped atop each other,
drowning tact and sensibility.
It floods like unchecked rage,
bruising the side
of a woman's cheek.
It floods like
          a memory.

Words

words find their way
into each crack;

they are dust motes
seen in the light;

words ride the waves
of blue-green seas,

wash up on shores
disguised as shells;

words are old bells
rung in town squares;

they are caskets,
grief for the lost;

words are the blood
in artists' veins,

permanent ink
for humankind.

Part IV:

Healing Stars

The Air Between Us

without the mixture of my molecules
and your molecules, the air is clearer,
fresher somehow, with a hint of jasmine,
pine, and tangerine—

without the verbal bullet holes and
the cock crowing, I can take a breath,
can spin around without hitting your ego,
fragile as it was—

without the rumbling of your empty
thunder, the sky has returned to me,
a prodigal piece of blessed haven,
draping me like a prayer

The Beginning of Me

I awoke in my body, but it wasn't my body
at least not the body I'd had before.
This was a new version, thinner, a little brittle
around the edges; everything ached with a weariness
I did not yet understand. But then, in the semi darkness
of the sterile room which smelled of disinfectant
and hospital linens, I remembered why I was here and
wondered what they'd written on my chart—nervous
breakdown? Hysteria? Woman gone completely mad?
No matter—time heals all wounds, or so they say,
something I'd never believed until now. The thought
made me smile, cracking my chapped lips, and I absently
traced a sunbeam splayed on the white cotton blanket,
feeling the first seedlings of hope sprout inside my chest.

The Brave Unbreakables

There's more than one way
to break a person

breaks that don't show up
in x-rays and are not bound
to bear a cast

breaks whose sharp edges
are concealed
within the confines of the heart

breaks that hide behind lying eyes,
that won't tumble from a tongue
but mumble, *It's OK. I'm fine*

and to those who bear such marks
but refuse to be statistics,
let us hold each other in solidarity

let us swear upon the blessed feet
of those who've come before us—
show them   they have not walked in vain.

The Breathing Hours

I slip into the midnight air,
relishing the sheen of sweat
shimmering on my half-clothed body;
August humidity seeps into my lungs,
and I feel at home with the sleek tree frogs.
Running to the dock, white-lace coverup
trailing behind like a wayward wedding veil.
I marvel at the waxing moon, just half a face
winking a solitary eye above my head.
As the lights of the house fade behind me,
I suppose I could be accused of snobbery,
selfishness even—but, in truth, I'm sloughing
off practiced pretense, the rules of social games
I've never wished to play. An introvert at heart,
I've shed my strappy dress, swapped it for a bathing suit
that allows my skin to breathe. No harm is intended
among the hobnobbing lake-goers at summer's end,
but I'll leave others to it—the glass raising, the dancing,
bonfires billowing smoke as raucous voices collide.
And I'll lie down on the swaying dock, drink the hoots
of the great horned owl, the crickets' chirp in the cattails,
and the lone cry of a coyote somewhere on the ridge.

City Oasis

The cacophony of honking taxis,
pedestrian crosswalks with millions
of talking heads,
jackhammers on concrete, and
the whistles of delivery drivers
smothers me like a plastic bag.
My breath coming in short gasps,
I wriggle through the sea of shoulders
and hail a bleating yellow beast.
To Central Park, I tell the driver,
a bit more rudely than I'd intended.
He drives in sacred silence, seeming
to understand my need for a reprieve.
Then I'm crossing the hallowed portal,
oak leaves swaying gently overhead,
a robin hopping across a pristine stretch
of luscious green grass.
I lower myself onto a bench
and close my eyes, inhaling, exhaling,
gently, rhythmically as a cool breeze
lifts the hair from my aching neck
and plants a kiss on my skin.

Finding space

on days when noises
fly in my face
like a murder of crows,
cawing and squawking,

when movements
flash around me,
disco balls slicing
every optic nerve,

when a touch
feels like spider webs,
and I propel both arms
in windmill defense,

I want to float,
to curve my body
like a spoon
against the dark side

of the slivered moon,
take measured breaths,
explore the silence
like one explores

the space left
by a pulled tooth,
close my eyes,
and drift into the abyss.

Gathering Minutes

the hands of the clock
move forward,
as do I—on autopilot;
24 hours in a day
is not enough
        to work
        to sleep
        to eat
        to live;
I want to grab
the minute hand,
caress it in my palm,
use it to stir a cup of tea,
use it to mark the pages
of a book,
hold it against my cheek
as I nap under a blanket;
I want to have a whole *pile*
of minutes,
enough to submerge
beneath in a tubful of bubbles,
enough to plant tulips deep in soil;
but I do what I can,
snatching song lyrics
from the passing breeze,
catching snowflakes on my tongue,
drawing hearts on frosted windowpanes.

I left God

beneath soiled linen
and balled up tissues.
Like a toddler in a tantrum,
I covered my ears
after I heard the diagnosis
and timeline of my life.
Between treatments,
my head above the toilet,
the only prayer that escaped
my lips was *Why?*
I didn't raise my hands to God
in praise or adoration
but to show him clumps of hair
mixed with peach shampoo.
The preacher came to see me
asked, are you a firm believer?
I said I used to be, and he said,
Why not now?
I told him I was angry; he said
that didn't change God's power.
He was still the great physician,
still King upon the throne.
Then he lifted eyes to heaven
and asked God to fill my room
with His beloved presence,
to hold my hand and let me know
He'd never left my side.
I felt the brush of angel wings
and the faith of generations
calm my broken spirit
and take away my fear.

I'm Made of Decisions

Decisions lie between every rib,
determine the curve of my spine,
lie in the wrinkled valleys of my face,
reside in the scar on my chin.
Decisions, for better or worse,
stare back at me in the mirror,
throb in the arches of my feet,
sink deep into bones once broken.
Decisions camp out in my brain,
weighing down the hippocampus
with what ifs and if onlys, leaving
just enough space for future regrets.
Decisions creep onto my pillow,
slide silently into my dreams,
as if I need reminded
even in my sleep.

In spite of

sterile rooms,
tiled floors,
the scent of antiseptic
in the air,

in spite of tubes
and drains
and hands that turn me
in the dark,

the mountains lie
in giant triangles
just beyond
chilled window panes;

I have seen the glory
of the sun
throwing diamonds
on fresh-fallen snow;

I have inhaled
Balsam firs
and woodsmoke
curled from chimneys;

there was never a trail
too long, too high,
          still no trail
too long, too high—

so, day after day
I will rise;
I   will   rise.

Lotus Flowers

from the recesses of murky water,
you rise

a burst of glorious pink
upon a gray-green stage

the sun your spotlight,
your petals shyly unfold,

as if nakedness is not your nature,
as if you might reveal too much

as soft as baby's breath
you lie unfurled, vulnerable

perhaps only a few can understand
the bravery of your bloom,

those who have ascended from depths
equal to your own

Lunch Break

Trees made of concrete and steel,
never sway, never bend
                    even a little;
glassy leaves showcase city grime
perhaps birds still sing,
but who can hear their melodies
over the unholy din of honking,
bustling to and fro, shouting—
each voice more insistent
than the last,
                    and yet here
in these smog-filled wilds
lies a pristine roof garden,
a 9x9 full of curling green ferns,
stout elephant ears, sago palms,
hibiscus, and beautiful bromeliads.
And it's in this intentional clearing
that I slowly spread mustard on rye
then layer turkey, salami, and Swiss
in delightful little heaps, creating
the perfect deli sandwich.
Then I stretch out on the wicker
chaise lounge, take my first bite,
and sigh with contentment
as the chickadees gather around me
cheeping for their crumbs.

Momma Needs a Moment

Just five minutes to close my eyes,
to allow my chest to rise and fall,
to let my mind go blank.
Put your badgering on a shelf,
tuck those questions under your arms,
and just let   me   *be.*
I cannot answer the rapid-fire requests
that press into the gray matter of my brain
like bullish thumbs against a tender wrist.
I cannot tell you what's for dinner.
No, I don't know where birds go
when they leave their nests.
I don't know why the store
was completely out of grapes.
Just let me have this bubble;
I'll close my eyes and imagine,
            if only for a moment
that I have all the space I need.
I'll stretch my arms over my head,
                        yawn,
listen to the coo of doves,
step into the sun's warm orb,
and measure my brief autonomy
in the beat of a hummingbird's wings.

My dog will get me

when I slowly rise from the bed,
each joint creaking
like a scarcely-oiled tin man;
he'll lift his silken head
from his place on the duvet,
knowing it will take me
a few more minutes to walk
toward the kitchen cupboards
to make my tea and his breakfast;
when I stay in my tattered nighty
until midday, his kind brown eyes
will not judge, not even with my hair
yet uncombed, my teeth unbrushed;
we'll putter around the garden,
looking for ripe tomatoes,
the only veggie I can still pick
without throwing my back out of kilter;
we'll doze in the recliner after lunch
probably in the middle of a game show;
when I awake, I'll search for my glasses,
and he'll wait patiently, ears perked
for my shout of glee when I find them
atop my head; he'll understand when
I'm out of dog biscuits and milk
and wag his tail when I promise
he can tag along to the grocer tomorrow;
should I grow melancholy, he'll place
his paw on my arm and sigh in solidarity.

My Father's Son

He wanted a son, he said.
So, I learned to pitch a ball
better than the great Cy Young.
He sighed when he gathered
fishing poles from the garage,
but I could hook a worm,
cast my line, reel in a fish,
and out-catch him any day.
He grumbled over yard work,
never acknowledging it was me
who did the clipping
and the mowing and the weeding.
He wanted a son, he said.
I wore a baseball cap—backwards,
I spit and swore and played poker.
When my mother died, I took over
the house—my brawny arms adept
for every chore, for cast iron skillet
dinners. Years later, as he lay dying,
my father whispered through his dry
cracked lips, *I'm glad you were my son.*

Reprieve

I sink into the sofa,
letting my arms fall
limply to each side.
Head back,
eyes closed
I breathe in the stillness,
allowing it to fill my lungs.
Upon release,
I feel the tension leave
my body,
the pressing weight
of children,
today's dinner menu,
dishes—laundry.
In that one moment,
I let it all go—
ease my shoulders
down,
tell myself
it's OK to be still,
to simply exist
in this tiny pocket
of time.

Rewilding

You were never one
to relax
to laugh unnecessarily—
always the gardener,
the trimmer,
and me your rose
not a stem or leaf
out of place.
You wanted me there
on that white trellis,
predictably climbing
always angled,
a strategic arrangement—
a display your guests
would gush about,
oh, what lovely roses!
You would smile
demurely—never
with too many teeth.
But I was not made
for gardens, for trellises,
for pruning and such.
So, I simply climbed
down—began to run
amuck, threading
through the begonias
creeping toward the ferns.

Soon, I was untamable,
peddling petals
in the long lemon grass.
Finally, you put away
your sheers, left me
to tend to myself,
and I ran stark naked
through the cow pasture;
I swear you wouldn't
recognize me
with clover in my hair.

Self-Care

stretching like a calico cat,
languid in the mellow bars

of sunshine drawing slanted
stripes across cotton sheets,

I revel in this weightless space
where time has been wrangled

into a pale, abstract shape;
there's no construct for meals,

for clothing beyond well-worn
shorts and the ratty t-shirt

I wore to bed, no insistent itch
to jump into the deep end

of a day—just nebulous clouds
of choices floating lazily

above my bed-head hair.

She Sang for Herself

She threaded music
through the fronds,
a seamstress with the voice
of a silver-throated angel;
she sang not for the ocean,
not for the palms,
not for the million grains of sand;
she sang not for the pelicans,
not for the gray-white gulls,
not for the sinking sun;
her arms open wide,
her head toward the sky,
she sang for her unruly curls,
she sang for her smooth brown skin,
she sang for her fingers and her toes,
for she did not owe a soul
the essence of her being;
she sang   she sang   she sang;
she sang a song for herself.

The Skin I'm In

all glass and steel and stone,
sharp edges that say,
stay over there;
I refract light,
deflect questions;
no one sees past
opaque windowpanes.
But inside—
          but inside—
I am tall, white-barked
birch trees,
birds on branches
trilling lullabies
to their babies:
I am liquid moon
poured into a pond,
crickets crying
in the cattails.
          Inside
I am home.

Time-Outs

we seek the unfindable,
those moments
just out of reach—

beyond honking traffic,
the clicking of shoes
on pavement;

and we know,
we just *know*
when we see them,

that lone golden leaf
lying on a sidewalk,
face up, dotted
with bubbles of rain

or the tenuous notes
of a sweet violin,
its owner bedraggled,
a cup at his feet,

or the rust-red glow
of the setting sun,
caught between high rises,
caught between our breaths

or the first snowflakes
of winter, iridescent
in the glow of streetlamps,
hushing the world

with their feathered weight.

An Unburdening

I picked up my stress,
felt the weight of it,
struggled to stay upright;
it seemed heavier
than last time—or
had I grown weaker?

I lay down with my stress,
felt the fear of it,
my eyes wide open,
helplessly awake
in the long, cruel hours
between night and dawn.

I worked with my stress,
felt the sharp edges,
as I bumped into it
with my hips, my shins,
leaving bruises
I could never quite explain.

I peeled away my stress,
left it lying there empty
like the skin of snake
and walked away,
bubbles of laughter popping
in a newly defiant mouth.

Part V:

Nature's Stars

Hibernation

I will pretend it's winter,
pretend I am a bear,
padding my cave with tufts
of mossy memories,
extra fat nestled inside
every cell for warmth
and survival;
I am not a quitter
but a respite seeker.
Behind closed eyelids,
behind the blue-white
sheets of snow,
I will rest, renew, restore
a heart
that holds the seeds
of spring.

Just the Bare Bones

Give me naked trees,
branches scraping
against winter's
steel-wool sky.

Give me a meadow
fat with clover,
bursting with pollen-
ladened bees.

Give me the tears
shed by a new widow,
her solitary cup
at odds with the table.

Give me a child,
mouth wide open
to receive the gift
of fresh snowflakes.

I'll hold the bones
of each tableau,
a rib here, a fibula there
until the whole skeleton

stands like a poem,
and walks away,
skull grinning

Latitude and Longitude

if I were to search the earth,
trot the entire globe
          for *peace,*
where would I find it?
could I put a pin there,
a shiny red pin,
on those north-south, east-west
coordinates
so that anytime
peace drained through the sieve
of my life,
I would simply make my way back
to that spot on the map,
36 degrees north, 81 degrees west,
that place where I met the sky
and hugged the milky way,
where I lay down
on garden-green earth
and breathed in the remnants
of all who had gone before me,
where I simultaneously
felt big and small on the mountaintop,
a gift from gods and eagles.

Lessons from the Moon

I'm so thin, I said to him,
the man in the moon,
and he smiled down at me,
and said: It's only a phase,
you'll see.
But my light is nearly out,
what shall I do in the dark?
Do? Why that's when you
          become new,
                    and life begins again.

Nature Speaks

There is a silence that seeps
into the world
only when humans are quiet,
only when they willingly cease
muttering and mucking about,
and it is in this silence
that I sit, knees drawn up to chin,
making myself as small as possible
beneath a canopy of ancient oaks,
listening to nature's voice
lifted in song from the beaks
of red-breasted robins,
skittering through the underbrush
on the bottom of chipmunk feet,
snapping dry branches
as a brown doe makes her way
to a sweet-clover clearing.
Even the leaves speak,
a simple shh-shh-shh
borne upon the autumn wind,
and I inhale and exhale,
matching Nature's unhurried breath.

The Ocean Gets Me

Unrefined,
unpretentious,
hair knotted,
clamped back
into a frizzy ball,
make-up free face
crusted with a fine sheen
of sweat and salt;
this is me—untamed,
punch-drunk on waves,
whooping with seagulls,
tan legs stretched out
on pristine white sand,
the smell of coconut oil,
Jimmy Buffet songs
airborne on the breeze;
I'll leave here today
after the ocean has swallowed
the sun—after my soul is saturated
with the holy balm of surf and sea.

Ode to Autumn

I lean back in the tree swing
my face tilted to a jewel-blue sky,
the dappled sun filtering through
a canopy of red and golden leaves.
I've become a child again,
delighting in the simple things,
the crisp air against my cheeks,
the muted smell of wood smoke
from collective chimneys.
There's a rhythm to autumn, the V
of geese, the rumble of machines
bringing in a king's treasury of corn,
animals nestling down in burrows,
preparing for the cold to come.
I ease into that rhythm,
slow down the pace of summer,
wrap myself in flannel, and make
hot chocolate on the stove.

One More Breath

Before my arthritic bones ache
from the frosty morning chill,
before I slip my body into fleece
and flannels,
before the leaves skitter off like kittens
across the browning hills,
give me one more breath of summer,
one more bath in bubbles of sunshine,
one more chance to dance under fairy lights
and pretend the begonias are still in bloom.

Six-Hundred Days of January

the sky flatlines—
ashes in a fireplace
        gone cold,
bare branches scrape
the windows,
begging to be spared
another layer of ice;
        the wind howls,
with rage
with loneliness,
no one knows;
        people press
against it,
seal their lips,
bundle scarves more tightly
around their bluish necks;
        holidays are in the rearview,
baubles tucked away in boxes;
the absence of color
reflecting in every hollow face.

To Shed a Season

to let leaves fall,
pile at your feet like red wool,
to sigh with the chilled wind,
—to let the fragile frost
creep over your heart,
a thin layer of diamonds
silver in the morning sun

to let gray clouds move in
and snowflakes pile atop
your head—to bury yourself
in the stillness, to practice
the pause that only winter
can bring, to hibernate
beneath your flannels

to open your windows
to birdsong—to catch golden
rays on eyelashes just opened,
to touch tender buds and revel
in the pale greenness of new life,
to press lips to daffodils, a nod
to fresh beginnings

Waiting for Rain

The smell of petrichor
hangs heavy in the air
like tender fruit
ripe for the picking.
Purple-bruised clouds
cluster together
as if for prayer,
as if they've heard
my placating voice
pinging through the heavens.
For it's not just the packed earth
that cracks its lips in supplication,
crying out for rain,
but my dusty soul,
the desert upon which lies
brick-oven grass,
How long must I wait?
How many times must I hear
the rumble of distant thunder
only to have it slip away,
pour its blessing
upon a foreign field?
I want to gather these plum clouds
like a bouquet of asters,
want to squeeze them
against my chest
until they give up solace
so long withheld.

What the Drought Leaves Behind

blooms
    once blood red,
    amethyst and tangerine,
    canary yellow, tutu pink,
    white as a wedding dress,
each gracing stems of green,
seducing bees
who become punch drunk
on nectar then fly away
with pollen-laden legs
blooms
    tubes and hearts
    petaled faces
    curled liked eyelashes
    vining over edges
each sucking drops of rain
calling to hummingbirds
who drink, mid-air, wings
beating to a frantic drum
before darting back to the trees
blooms
    drooping in summer heat
    gasping for moisture, for rain
    that never comes,
    turning brown beneath
    a brutal sun, bleached of color
each one dying on their stems,
fading like lost memories
mourned by bees
deserted by birds
they shrivel on brittle stems.

When Frogs Are Put to Bed

Moisture spills from unbuttoned clouds
kissing the grass with diamond lips;
there's silence in the wood-scented air—
the absence of geese flown south,
the absence of frogs nestled in mud,
the absence of cricket violins now tucked
away in miniature cases;
the hum of summer over,
leaves fall to the ground
like golden-red confetti
and the north wind sweeps
them away with a swoosh
of her new winter broom.

Winter Dream

My eyes grow heavy with sleep
in the late afternoon hours
where the pale grayish light
has not ceased to be gray
for one-hundred days it seems.
Head sinking into the soft folds
of the sofa,
I wander across an expansive lawn
filled with clover and dandelions.
The bees are euphoric,
a little drunk, I think,
as they drift lazily
from blossom to blossom
like tiny yellow-brown clouds.
I stretch out, cat-like, in the grass,
feeling its carpet-softness
beneath my bare brown legs.
Then from a branch above my head,
a mother robin swoops down,
scolding and scolding
as she hops and bobs frantically
about ten paces away.
I understand what she is saying,
Don't bother my babies!
Don't bother my babies!
I laugh and tell her they are safe,
as I'm still trapped in a snow globe.

Winter's Gift

slowing down,
          emptying myself
like brown molasses
poured from a glass jug,
the rise and fall
of my chest
          deliberate,
each breath
calculated,
held—released;
snowflakes fall
outside the chilled
windowpane,
          fairy dust
in the white-walled wind,
and it's this quite seclusion
that insulates my body,
          my brain,
this natural phenomenon
that buries trails,
cuts off passes,
          covers roads,
that offers, instead, quilts,
the aroma of coffee beans,
and a book too delicious
to put down.

Part VI:

Laughing Stars

Anti-Aging

I throw a couple more bottles
of anti-aging cream into the trash.
They're outdated now, like me.
Too old to be effective.
I'm not sure why I keep ordering
such products. Advertising genius,
I suppose. Those clever little videos
that show women with crepey necks
rubbing on this and that until suddenly—
their necks look twenty years younger.
Perhaps I'm just an anomaly—having
one of those stubborn necks that defy
all attempts to erase the natural
indentations of time—or the videos
are fake, little tricks of technology
designed to extract a few more dollars
from my thinning wallet.
I'm done being fooled. Being a fool.
Aging is inevitable. But wait—
what is this on my phone? Organic,
whipped beef tallow? I'll take two.

How to Eat an Over-Easy Egg in Front of Your Ex

carefully,
deliberately,
fork cutting
straight down the middle,
yolk pooling
like a daisy-yellow pond,
perfect for dipping
butter-covered toast;
fold the bread,
drag it along the plate
in slow, circular motions,
absorbing,
never dripping—
never leaving the table
with egg on your face

Middle-Age Monotony

creaking like an un-greased porch swing,
each bone protesting forward movements,
too stiff
too sore
one foot in front of the other,
one hand caressing an aching hip;
why do bodies give up so easily
when the heart is still throwing confetti
like it's New Year's Eve?

No Filet Mignon for Me

I'd butchered the English essay,
but my professor had left the blood,
red ink spilled across each page in a
tsunami of comments and corrections.
Lord knows I'd tried to wrestle the meat
out of Edward Thomas's poem "Birds'
Nests," but I had apparently sprained
my arm in the process, inadequately
sucking the marrow of metaphorical
nuances. So, sorry, Miss Professor
that I didn't filet the tender flank
of seasonal allusions and marinate it
with the tender juices of passing time.
Please excuse my oversight, the use
of too much gristle skidding through the
perfect cut of prime like polished shoes
on parched linoleum—guess I didn't notice
the boy in the poem suffered so much from
nostalgia and regret. I see now that sirloin
wasn't exactly my finest choice, what with
the overcooked mention of leaves and jays.
Next time I'll use a sharper knife, and perhaps
you could use different colored ink?

Not in the Same Way

I love you.
Not in the same way
I love pizza, of course.
Or the sun on my face.
Or the sound of birdsong.
But I love you.
Not in the same way
I love a rainy day
and a good book.
Or cute puppies.
Or chocolate cake.
But I love you.
Not in the same way
I love thrift shopping.
Or the perfect May day.
Or comfortable shoes.
But I love you.
Not in the same way
I love fuzzy blankets.
Or essential oils.
Or a hot shower.
But I love you.
And that counts
for something.

Roomba Rumble

I thought I'd like an auto vacuum—
I mean what with the reviews and all.
What a relief it would be not to sweep,
and bend and gather bits and pieces into dustpans.
Like a kid at Christmas, I unwrap the package,
read the instructions, and send little Ruby Roomba
(that's what I name her) on her way across the floor.
I squeal when she turns, when she bumps against
the dog crate and turns again. Such a clever girl!
For months we live in harmony—she pulls her weight,
gobbles up her share of dirt and crumbs left behind
by a romping family. But upon returning home one day,
I gasp to see Ruby butting her head against the wall.
Over and over she crashes as though possessed, so
I nudge her with my foot, hoping to quiet her tantrum,
but I swear, she *turns* on me—runs onto my foot,
tries to climb my leg! I shake off the rabid beast,
flip her on her back until she lies uselessly spinning,
spinning, gasping as dust motes settle on her belly.

Social Hoo-Hahs

It’s the one party everyone is talking about,
the one even the Commander is attending,
and you, wife of a colonel, are expected
to attend—so, you fret about the dress,
(should you wear a dress or nice slacks?),
fret about the height of the heels,
whether to wear your hair up or down—
but really you fret about the hobnobbing,
the incessant grinning and sugar-sweet
politeness that will make your entire face
feel like it’s cracking by night’s end,
and your feet will hurt (regardless of the shoe
choice)—and you’ll attempt to escape
to some bland outdoor patio to dull the thumping
in your head, but before you can draw a breath,
you’ll hear a voice—Darling! There you are!
Why are you standing alone in the dark?

Triggers

a laugh
a sneeze
a cough
a trickle of warmth
between my legs
the betrayal of a bladder
weak from the children
who once borrowed my womb;
thank God for fashionable
diapers, the security blanket
for a body gone rogue with age.

About the Author

Arvilla Fee lives in Dayton, Ohio with her husband, three of her six children, and her two dogs, Max & Scooter. She teaches English for Clark State College and is the lead poetry editor for *October Hill Magazine.*

She has published poetry, photography, and short stories in over 100 publications, including *North of Oxford, Cholla Needles, Mudlark, Tipton Poety Journal, Rye Whiskey Review,* and *The Orchards Poetry Journal.* Her poetry books, *The Human Side, This is Life,* and *Mosaic: A Million Little Pieces,* are available through Wipf and Stock and Amazon.

Arvilla loves writing, photography, and traveling and never leaves home without a snack and water (just in case of an apocalypse). She writes to make sense of the world around her and often uses writing in a therapeutic way to express trauma, grief, and pain. Her goal is to make poetry accessible to everyone and to give people a voice when they cannot find the words they wish to say. Arvilla hopes that through her writing readers of all ages and walks of life are able to find connections, see parts of themselves in the pages of her books, and know they are not alone. To learn more about Arvilla, visit her website.

Check out her online poetry magazine:
soulpoetry7.com

www.ingramcontent.com/pod-product-compliance
Lightning Source LLC
LaVergne TN
LVHW090610110826
845146LV00001B/328

* 9 7 9 8 9 0 1 4 6 8 6 1 6 *